COOKING
AROUND THE WORLD

A Chinese Cookbook for Kids

Rosemary Hankin

PowerKiDS
press.
New York

Published in 2014 by The Rosen Publishing Group, Inc.
29 East 21st Street, New York, NY 10010

Produced for Rosen by Calcium Creative Ltd
Editor for Calcium Creative Ltd: Sarah Eason
US Editor: Sara Howell
Designer: Paul Myerscough

Photo credits: Cover: Shutterstock: Wavebreakmedia. Inside: Dreamstime: Pipa100 7l, Yurchyk 7r; Shutterstock: 54613 10, 29tr, Awei 25t, Beboy 5tl, Dionisvera 13b, Dotweb Steen B Nielsen 18, 29tr, Hart Photography 6, Heinteh5 22, 28l, Pius Lee 9t, Richard M Lee 1, 14, 26, 28br, 29b, MJ Prototype 9b, Sunday Morning 13t, Photo-oasis 5b, Stephen Rudolph 17t, Elena Schweitzer 21t, Svry 25b, ValeStock 21b, Yuri Yavnik 5tr, Claudio Zaccherini 17b.

Library of Congress Cataloging-in-Publication Data

Hankin, Rosemary.
 A Chinese cookbook for kids / by Rosemary Hankin.
     pages cm. — (Cooking around the world)
 Includes index.
 ISBN 978-1-4777-1335-8 (library binding) — ISBN 978-1-4777-1518-5 (pbk.) — ISBN 978-1-4777-1519-2 (6-pack)
 1. Cooking, Chinese—Juvenile literature. I. Title.
 TX724.5.C5H348 2014
 641.5951—dc23
                                   2013003363

Manufactured in the United States of America

CPSIA Compliance Information: Batch #S13PK8: For Further Information contact Rosen Publishing, New York, New York at 1-800-237-9932

Contents

Discover China

China is the biggest country in Asia and the fourth-largest country in the world. For each American, there are five Chinese people. That is a lot of people!

China has mountains, **deserts**, and **tropical forests**. Mount Everest is found in the Himalayas between China and Nepal. It is the world's tallest mountain and is 29,035 feet (9 km) high. China has three great rivers. They are the Yellow River, the Yangtze River, and the Pearl River.

The Chinese have a saying, "Food is heaven for the people," and it is important to them to eat good food with family and friends. Different areas of China have different ways of cooking. There are dishes that were created for the **emperors** who ruled China long ago. There are even dishes that are designed just to be good for your health!

Rice is grown on flooded farmland, called paddy fields.

The Great Wall of China was built around 2,000 years ago. It is more than 4,000 miles (6,400 km) long.

Texture, or how food feels in your mouth, is important in Chinese cooking. This dish combines soft pork fat and crunchy bean sprouts.

Get Set to Cook

Cooking is fun! There is nothing better than making food and then sharing it with your family and friends.

Every recipe page in this book starts with a "You Will Need" list. This is a set of **ingredients**. Be sure to collect everything on the list before you start cooking.

Look out for the "Top Tips" boxes. These have great tips to help you cook.

"Be Safe!" boxes warn you when you need to be extra careful.

Use one cutting board for meat and fish and a different cutting board for vegetables and fruit.

Always ask a grown-up if you can do some cooking.

Watch out for sharp knives! Ask a grown-up to help you with chopping and slicing.

Be sure to wash your hands before you start cooking.

Always wash any fruit and vegetables before using them.

Always ask a grown-up for help when cooking on the stove or using the oven.

Wear an apron to keep your clothes clean as you cook.

Beijing Style

Northern Chinese cooking is a range of cooking styles that have been mixed together. They include traditional Chinese cooking and dishes that were brought to China by the **Mongols**, who were **invaders** from other areas of Asia. Dishes from northern China are often light and tasty.

Food for Emperors

Beijing is the capital of China. It was once the Imperial City, where the emperors of China lived. The emperors had very good **chefs** who came from all over China and brought their own ways of cooking with them. The emperors' chefs worked hard to make dishes that their masters would like. Their most famous dish is Peking duck.

Everyday Meals

Corn is grown in northern China, but the main crop is wheat. The local people eat wheat noodles. They also like pancakes, which are eaten with both sweet and **savory** fillings. Leeks, scallions, and garlic are used in many dishes.

The Imperial Palace is in the Forbidden City, in Beijing. The city was built between the thirteenth and seventeenth centuries.

People in northern China love noodles served with pork.

Corn Soup

YOU WILL NEED:

1 x 15 ounce (425 g) can
    creamed corn
2¼ cups chicken stock
1 tbsp cornstarch
2 tbsp water
1 egg, beaten
salt and ground white
    pepper, to taste

People have been making corn into soup since ancient times. The Aztecs, ancient Egyptians, and the Chinese all made it. Corn soup can be savory or sweet. You can also add seafood such as crab meat or shrimp.

BE SAFE!
- Be careful when you open the can of corn.
- Ask a grown-up to help you make the chicken stock if you are using a bouillon cube.

STEP 1

In a saucepan, combine the creamed corn and chicken stock. Bring to a boil over medium-high heat. Stir occasionally with a spoon.

STEP 2

In a small bowl or cup, use a spoon to mix together the cornstarch and water until you have made a smooth paste.

STEP 3

Pour the cornstarch mixture into the boiling corn soup, stirring all the time. Continue cooking and stirring for around 2 minutes, or until the soup has thickened fully.

STEP 4

Now, gradually add the beaten egg, stirring all the time. The egg will break up into fine strands in the soup. Add salt and ground white pepper, to taste. Remove the soup from the heat and serve while hot.

Southern Cooking

The Chinese food you love is probably Cantonese, which is a style of cooking that comes from southern China. When people from southern China moved to the United States and Europe, they took their cooking with them, and it soon became popular!

Healthy Food

Cantonese dishes are light, healthy, and full of great flavor. Cooks like to steam and **stir-fry** their food. This means they do not need to use a lot of oil as they cook. The finished dishes have pretty garnishes, such as radish and carrot flowers.

Wonderful Weather

The south of China has rich soil which is good for growing crops such as sweet potatoes, mangoes, and **lychees**. There are rice paddy fields in the Pearl River **delta**. Beef cattle, pigs, and chickens are raised here. Fish and seafood are also used in Cantonese cooking.

Lovely Flavors

Soy and ginger are used in many Cantonese dishes, along with oyster sauce and mushroom sauce. Black beans and shrimp paste are used to add a rich flavor.

Chinese cooks often steam food in bamboo containers. It is a very healthy way to cook.

Fresh ginger contains lots of vitamin C and is very good for you. It also adds a delicious flavor to many dishes.

13

Egg Fried Rice

YOU WILL NEED:

1 egg
2 tsp sesame oil
2 tbsp vegetable oil
1 cup long grain rice
   (dry measure), cooked
1 cup frozen peas, defrosted
4 scallions, finely chopped
1–2 tsp **soy sauce**
ground white pepper,
   to taste

Egg fried rice is easy to make. It is a meal on its own and you can add extra ingredients, too. For the best results, cook the rice and cool completely before frying. That way it won't stick together.

BE SAFE!
• Ask a grown-up to help you cook the rice.
• Be careful when chopping the scallions.

STEP 1

Beat together the egg and sesame oil and set aside.

STEP 2

Heat the vegetable oil in a wok or large pan. When really hot, add the rice and stir-fry for around 3–4 minutes until hot.

STEP 3

Add the peas and scallions. Stir-fry, turning the rice constantly, for around 3 minutes. **Season** well with soy sauce and ground white pepper. Then push the mix to one side of the pan.

STEP 4

Tip the pan slightly. Pour the beaten egg mixture into the empty half of the pan. Leave for around 10 seconds so it begins to set. Then, using chopsticks, toss the egg with the rice, breaking the egg up. Stir-fry for another minute and serve immediately.

Largest City

Shanghai is on the east coast of China. It is the largest city in the country and over 23 million people live there. There are many restaurants in Shanghai. There are also lots of street food stalls that sell steamed stuffed buns, dumplings, and wontons.

Red Cooking

Shanghai cooks use lots of soy sauce, sugar, rice wine, and rice vinegar. "Red cooking" is a famous method of cooking that comes from Shanghai. In red cooking, food is slowly cooked in a mixture of soy sauce, sugar, and often five-spice powder. Many Shanghai families have their own secret recipes for red cooking, and they are kept a close secret!

The Mighty Yangtze

The Yangtze River flows out into the East China Sea at Shanghai. It is the longest river in Asia and is 3,915 miles (6,300 km) long. There are lots of freshwater fish in the Yangtze. The river also has large **floodplains** on which rice is grown. This area around the Yangtze is known as "the land of fish and rice," and these are the foods that most local dishes are cooked with.

The Yangtze River provides many freshwater fish. Fishermen make their catch from traditional boats using nets or hooks.

Delicious, colorful snacks are sold at Shanghai street stalls.

Lion's Head Meatballs

YOU WILL NEED:

1 pound (453 g) ground pork

5 canned water chestnuts, finely chopped

1 tsp ginger root, finely chopped

1 small onion, finely chopped

2 tbsp soy sauce

1 egg, beaten

2 tbsp cornstarch

2 tbsp vegetable oil

1¼ cups chicken stock

½ tsp sugar

4 ounces (113 g) scallions, trimmed

salt and ground black pepper, to taste

These large meatballs are very, very tasty. The meatballs look like a lion's head and the greens are meant to be the lion's mane. They are fun to cook and great to eat!

BE SAFE!
- Be careful when chopping the vegetables.
- Ask a grown-up to make the stock using a bouillon cube or powder.

18

STEP 1

Mix the pork, water chestnuts, ginger, and onion in a bowl. Add the soy sauce and beaten egg. Form into evenly sized meatballs. Roll them in the cornstarch.

STEP 2

Heat the oil in a wok. Brown the meatballs, turning them occasionally. Add the stock and sugar. Season with salt and ground black pepper, to taste. Stir, then cover and simmer for 20–25 minutes.

STEP 3

Increase the heat and add the scallions. Cook for 3–4 minutes, or until the scallions are just wilted.

STEP 4

Remove the scallions from the pan and arrange on a warmed serving dish. Top with the meatballs and pour the sauce over.

Nice and Spicy

Cooks in southwest China have a style of cooking called Szechuan. It uses mainly chili paste and dried chilies, garlic, and ginger. Special chili pepper oil adds a strong flavor to many dishes.

Bigger and Bigger

Chongqing is a city in southwest China. It is also the fastest-growing city in the world. Half a million people move there every year! This ancient city began 3,000 years ago and it is known for the hot, spicy food that is sold in its restaurants and street food stalls.

Chinese New Year

The Chinese have many **festivals** every year. Spring Festival, when Chinese New Year is celebrated, is the most important. It begins in late January or early February and continues for two weeks. It includes parades, lion and dragon dances, feasts, and fireworks. Spring Festival ends with the Lantern Festival, which takes place when the first full moon of the year appears.

Chilies, dried and fresh, are used in Szechuan cooking.

秘制烤山鸡 香酥鹌
15元1只 6

Many food stalls can be found under one roof in this food hall. People pick and choose their food, then sit at the tables to eat.

21

Spring Rolls

YOU WILL NEED:

3 ounces (85 g) rice noodles
vegetable oil
9 ounces (255 g) ground pork
1 small onion, finely chopped
2 garlic cloves, minced
½ inch piece ginger root,
   peeled and finely grated
1 carrot, peeled and grated
5 ounces (141 g) button
   mushrooms, finely chopped
1 cup white cabbage, chopped
1½ tbsp soy sauce
11 ounce (311 g) packet frozen
   spring roll pastry, thawed

These little food "parcels" are made to celebrate Chinese New Year. This takes place in the spring, and that is how the rolls got their name! They were first made using fresh vegetables. Today, spring rolls may contain meat and seafood, too.

BE SAFE!
- Be careful around boiling water.
- Ask a grown-up to help you prepare the vegetables.

STEP 1

In a heatproof bowl, cover the noodles with boiling water. Let stand for 5 minutes. Drain and cool. Chop the noodles and place in a mixing bowl.

STEP 2

Heat 2 tbsp of oil in a skillet. Add the pork and **sauté**, stirring occasionally until browned. Add to the noodles.

STEP 3

Heat 1 tbsp of oil in the same pan. Add the onion, garlic, and ginger. Cook, stirring occasionally, until soft. Add the carrots, mushrooms, and cabbage. Cook until tender. Add to the noodles. Stir in the soy sauce. Refrigerate.

STEP 4

Preheat the oven to 400°F (200°C). Place a pastry wrap on your work surface, with one corner pointing toward you. Place a heaping tablespoon of the filling on the near corner. Brush the pastry edges with water. Roll up, folding in the edges. Repeat for each roll.

STEP 5

Place the spring rolls on a lined baking sheet. Brush them with vegetable oil then bake the rolls in the oven for 25 minutes.

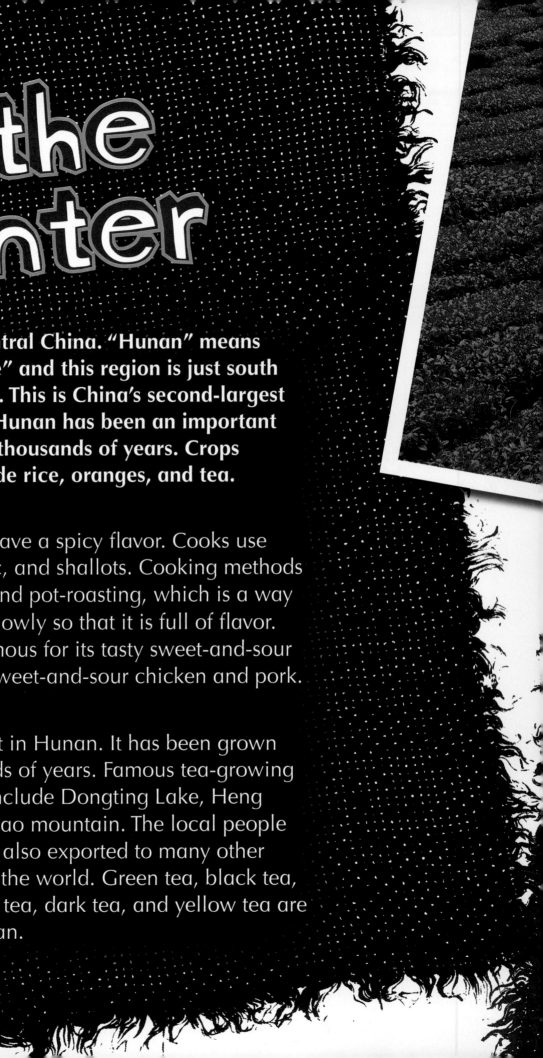

In the Center

Hunan is in central China. "Hunan" means "south of the lake" and this region is just south of Dongting Lake. This is China's second-largest freshwater lake. Hunan has been an important farming area for thousands of years. Crops grown here include rice, oranges, and tea.

Sweet and Sour

Hunan dishes have a spicy flavor. Cooks use lots of chili, garlic, and shallots. Cooking methods include stewing and pot-roasting, which is a way of cooking food slowly so that it is full of flavor. Hunan is also famous for its tasty sweet-and-sour recipes, such as sweet-and-sour chicken and pork.

Land of Tea

Tea is important in Hunan. It has been grown there for thousands of years. Famous tea-growing areas in Hunan include Dongting Lake, Heng mountain, and Shao mountain. The local people drink tea and it is also exported to many other countries all over the world. Green tea, black tea, white tea, oolong tea, dark tea, and yellow tea are all grown in Hunan.

Tea plantations cover the hills of central China. The leaves are picked by hand.

Sweet-and-sour food is a favorite in Hunan. Dishes are sweet and spicy, but not too hot.

25

Sweet-and-Sour Chicken

YOU WILL NEED:

⅓ cup rice vinegar
4 tbsp brown sugar
1 tbsp ketchup
4 tsp water
1 tsp soy sauce
2 tsp cornstarch
2 scallions, sliced
1 red bell pepper,
  finely chopped
1 packet chicken nuggets

This is a really quick and easy Chinese meal. Make a tasty sweet-and-sour sauce and serve it with your favorite chicken nuggets or other oven-baked chicken pieces.

BE SAFE!
• Be careful when you are slicing and chopping the vegetables.
• Ask a grown-up to help you when baking the chicken nuggets.

STEP 1

Preheat the oven following the instructions on the packet for the chicken nuggets. Place the chicken nuggets on a baking sheet and bake according to the instructions.

STEP 2

Meanwhile, in a pan, mix together the rice vinegar, brown sugar, ketchup, and soy sauce. Bring to a boil.

STEP 3

With a spoon, mix the cornstarch with 4 tsp water in a small bowl or cup until smooth. Add the mixture to the pan, stirring until thickened.

STEP 4

Remove the chicken nuggets from the oven and toss them in the sweet-and-sour sauce. Quickly stir in the scallions and red bell pepper. Put the chicken on a serving dish. Serve with rice or noodles.

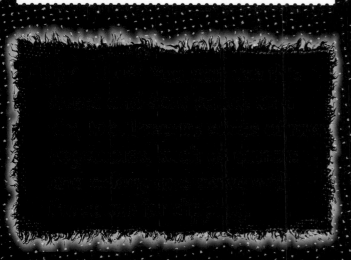

Chinese Meals on the Map!

Kazakhstan

Spring Rolls

Egg Fried Rice

Now that you have discovered the delicious foods of China and how to cook them, find out where they are cooked and eaten on this map of the country.

Corn Soup

Russia

Lion's Head
Meatballs

BEIJING

China

Shanghai

South China
Sea

Yangtze River

Hunan

Sweet-and-
Sour Chicken

Burma

Glossary

Aztecs (AZ-teks) People who created a great empire in Mexico hundreds of years ago.

chefs (SHEFS) People who are hired to cook food.

delta (DEL-tuh) A pile of earth and sand that collects at the mouth of a river.

deserts (DEH-zurtz) Areas that have almost no rain and so have very few plants.

emperors (EM-per-erz) People who rule huge areas of land.

festivals (FES-tih-vulz) Large celebrations in which many people take part.

floodplains (FLUD-playnz) Areas of land around a river that are covered with river water when a river floods.

garnish (GAR-nish) To decorate food before serving.

ingredients (in-GREE-dee-untz) Different foods and seasonings that are used to make a recipe.

invaders (in-VAYD-erz) People who travel to another country to try to take it over.

lychees (LEE-cheez) A type of pale, sweet-tasting fruit.

Mongols (MON-gulz) People from Mongolia in northern Asia.

sauté (saw-TAY) To lightly fry food in oil or butter.

savory (SAY-vuh-ree) Food that is not sweet in taste.

season (SEE-zun) To add flavor.

soy sauce (SOY SOS) A dark brown sauce that is made from soy beans and used in Chinese cooking.

stir-fry (STUR-fry) To cook food very quickly by frying it in a hot pan.

tropical forests (TRAH-puh-kul FOR-ests) Forests with a very high rainfall.

Further Reading

Colson, Mary. *Chinese Culture*. Global Cultures. Chicago: Heinemann-Raintree, 2013.

Crean, Susan. *Discover China*. Discover Countries. New York: PowerKids Press, 2012.

Lee, Frances. *The Young Chef's Chinese Cookbook*. I'm the Chef! New York: Crabtree Publishing, 2002.

Websites

Due to the changing nature of Internet links, PowerKids Press has developed an online list of websites related to the subject of this book. This site is updated regularly. Please use this link to access the list:

www.powerkidslinks.com/caw/chin

Index